THE CONVERSATION

Stephanie Norgate is a poet and playwright. Her plays have been broadcast on BBC Radio 4. For many years, she ran the MA in Creative Writing at Chichester University and is now a Royal Literary Fund Fellow. She edited an international collection of essays, *Poetry and Voice* (CSP, 2012) and Winchester Poetry Festival's Chalk Poets Anthology (Sarsen Press, 2015). In 2016, she completed a study of poetry trails for South Downs National Park. As a translator, she has contributed to *Modern Poetry in Translation* and the MPT anthology, *Centres of Cataclysm* (Bloodaxe Books/MPT, 2016). Her chapter about the imagery of the house in her poetry appears in *Architectural Space and the Imagination* (Palgrave Macmillan, 2020). Her three collections of poetry with Bloodaxe are *Hidden River* (2008), which was shortlisted for both the Forward Prize for Best First Collection and the Jerwood Aldeburgh First Collection Prize, *The Blue Den* (2012) and *The Conversation* (2021).

STEPHANIE NORGATE

The Conversation

BLOODAXE BOOKS

ISBN: 978 1 78037 574 8

First published 2021 by
Bloodaxe Books Ltd,
Eastburn,
South Park,
Hexham,
Northumberland NE46 1BS

www.bloodaxebooks.com
For further information about Bloodaxe titles
please visit our website and join our mailing list
or write to the above address for a catalogue.

Supported using public funding by
ARTS COUNCIL
ENGLAND

Cover design: Neil Astley & Pamela Robertson-Pearce.

Printed in Great Britain by Bell & Bain Limited, Glasgow, Scotland, on
acid-free paper sourced from mills with FSC chain of custody certification.

in memory of Helen Dunmore
and for my friends
may the conversation continue

ACKNOWLEDGEMENTS

Thanks are due to the editors of the following magazines, anthologies and websites: *And Other Poems, Barbican Newsletter, Bird Count November and Other Prose Poems* (Wild Mouse with Tongues & Grooves, 2018), *Chalk Poets* (Sarsen Press, 2016, for Winchester Poetry Festival and South Downs National Park Association), *The London Magazine, Mixed Borders* garden residencies online anthology (The Poetry School, 2015), *The Oxford Magazine, Poetry and All That Jazz* (Festival of Chichester anthologies, 2012-2020), *Plague20Journal, Poetry South East 2020* (Frogmore Press, 2020), *All My Important Nothings* (Smith | Doorstop, 2015), *Ten Poems about Walking* (Candlestick Press, 2019), *Staying Human* (Bloodaxe Books, 2020), Troubadour Coffee House website, *Where We Are Now* website. 'Sycamore' was commissioned by Winchester Poetry Festival and Hampshire Hospitals to display in waiting rooms (2016).

Thanks to the librarians, curators and trustees of the Otter Gallery, where I was poet in residence from 2010 to 2018. Thanks to the Weald and Downland Living Museum and South Downs Poetry Festival for inviting me to host poetry workshops. Thanks to the Poetry School, London Parks and Gardens and volunteers at the Fann Street Wildlife Garden, where I was poet in residence in 2015. Finally, thanks to the Royal Literary Fund for an RLF Fellowship at Southampton University which enabled me to complete this collection.

CONTENTS

The House

Don't tell me that you've never lingered
under the eaves of the mystery house,
wondering who lives there, conjuring their lives.

Don't tell me the house has never appeared to you
in the town's street or along a woodland lane,
where its windows throw out long squares of light.

It must be a cold night after a short day,
salt and grit glinting on pavements, ice thickening
on pot-holes. You will feel a little lonely,
between the now and the then, with the old life heard
away in the hills, a faint singing of owls.

Then the house will appear, grown in the gap,
hiding its gold behind gauze or linen,
until a figure opens the curtains, sees you standing there.

If you're brave, you'll step onto the night path,
leave your prints on thin snow and climb the steps
to the porch. At your knock, the door will open
to a room of talk, where last year's logs
hiss and silver in the blackening stove.

The old friends will be there saying, 'You're late.
We waited. Where were you?'

Eavesdroppers

Some stood beneath
the thatch, mouths open
drinking sweet drops
trickling from mould
or moss. Who ever thought
thirst would be dangerous,
like swallowing swords
or fire? Was it the thatch
or the wind in its quills,
that whistled the story
and watched the villagers
run after it, hungry
for a gleaning when harvest
was long over?

Word Hoards

Where curators or criminals of war
once hid works of art under mountains
among stalactites and stone curtains,
where men hacked out iron ore or coal,
or risked their lives for salt or gold,
down the widening shafts where miners
were lowered in lifts, they are lowering
the databases to be cooled by dark water,
down here where only the human fish
can listen to them hum and hiss.

But some rafts of data drift out to sea,
stored, offshore, tax free, cooled
by the rhythms of the thrifty waves.
Perhaps in these may be the electric sparks
we sent, the WikiLeaks, the coded bleeps,
the single *I*, the plural *you* and *they*,
the words spoken, even the words
unwise, unwished for, better left unwritten
and then so carefully deleted,
are rocked in storms, lulled in calms,
their ghost forms floating.

Miracle

In supermarkets, strapped
in a trolley,

on the motorway,
belted in the back of a car,

under the foundered houses,
open mouthed and fed by drips,

in a box drilled with holes
in the hold of a boat,

in fish crates and on cardboard,
on pallets and straw,

on a bed of needles
on the forest floor,

in the curve of a rosy scarf
tied to a woman's back,

in a line of walkers
along railway tracks,

under a tarpaulin
on mud and sand,

a child is sleeping,
a child is sleeping.

February Foxes

The foxes are out on the frozen pavements,
grown thin, foxed by the new bins.

They are pawing at someone's take-away silver,
licking the remains of curry, tasting red chicken.

We drive slowly the two miles to the hospital,
for you are ready to be born.

Foxes scavenge at each cross-roads
and roll on the frosty mica of the road.

They are the owners of the night's streets,
so starved they would eat your placenta if they could.

In the morning light, a few flakes
of snow fall, and you are in your cot,

tired from the journey,
and the foxes fade

to a dream of need, of the hunger
that nuzzles at tarmac, a kind of blessing

in the city's night, when the wild
can be born under the sodium lights.

Sycamore

After the queue for the car park, when you're fumbling
for change, you hear sycamore leaves scratch the tarmac.
They curl in on themselves, shuffle along the kerb,
rattle around your feet and over the white lines.
Then a breeze loosens the seeds from the trees,
and sycamore keys whirl groundwards.
You catch pairs of them as they twirl in the blue air
and smuggle them into your pocket together
with a red stemmed leaf, the deep gold of an ingot.

Once inside, you watch another sycamore
press its keys against hospital glass. Waiting
memorialises their brown paper bunches,
the coupling of their off-kilter half-moons,
the dry yearning after flight. You watch sunlight
light up the flittering edges of the tree's last leaves,
slow sugars burning to yellow. No food for a day.
You hear your name and slip your hand in your pocket
to touch the helicopter wings, before you go in.

Dead Nettle in the Fann Street Wildlife Garden

It doesn't sting and it isn't dead.
Instead, the dead nettle thinks itself
all over the grass, huddles with the cowslips,
nudges in with the ox-eye daisies,
and raises its estates of honeyed towers.

To show it lives in the blitzed earth,
the dead nettle grows from its square stem
calyces like struts for balconies
where green hearts leaf,
and white shirts billow over them.

Wildlife Garden in the City

Who will read
the garden's legend
as it rises out of the map
and plants itself at the pond's edge?

Water boatmen elbow drowned towers.
The Shakespeare lends no answer.

In Golden Lane,
goldfinches feed on mist, love, seed.

Men in hard hats shout
hey hatty hey and *look love look.*

A gleam, half dark, half rain
staggers and climbs. A stag
beetle in slow labour.

                    Soles
draw lines over the ox-eyed grass.

A wren sings to glass, to glass.

                    Who owns
the air's vibrato
when a bird's churr
rises above the machine's whirr?

The high life
renders rhythms over broken brickwork,
whistles down over tormentil and thistles.

A hiss quivers in the grass. An ash
shivers in the drilling.

Will streetlights
tell what they see, the wildering
saw-toothed, clawing and calling
the vixen into the city's den?

What ivy holds
is the root of secrets –

mesh of founderings, dust cloud houses,
foxing the margins of earth's rent.

outside some flats in Camberwell

white tape with red flashes
[   ] the scene
candlewax weeps
among flowers

white tape with red flashes
[   ] the scene
tough white tape
whipping out

to the street
[   ] his story
edging us round
to run on

Orthopaedics and Trauma, King's College Hospital

Waiting, we glimpse the blue
alternate world of surgeons in scrubs
wearing the cornflower hue

of calm lakes on hot days, slubs
of tracked water and boat trails,
while the receptionist rubs

the arm of the flirty male
guard, who sways her over the polished floor
to his reggae hum. The guard bails

out of their rhythm-tour
to grab his phone at the prisoner's call.
'He says he'll be free by four.

'He's asking for food. He's scared he'll fall.
He wants you to know he's been treated well.'
Later, the prisoner lurches against the wall,

arms tense on crutches, and the guards tell
him to go steady. He'll be okay.
Glass doors glide open to a swell

of heat. And here's our daughter in the doorway
with the surgeon who inspected the moon
of her patella, the spongy stay

of torn cartilage and the lock of bones.
They pack the prisoner in the van. We never know
where he goes. Our daughter swings over kerb stones.

In London parks, afternoon lawns glow
like the green scrubs of the young anaesthetist
who took my father's hands so long ago

and said, 'I'll see you through this.'
I wish he knew how his green grew over years,
five fields fed by the rain's promise.

Bedroom Tax

They want your sewing machine,
your desk, your shelf of books, your table.
They want your toolbox and your woodwork bench.
They want the playdough and the easel,
the Lego and the guitar strings.

They'll come for the view, the dapple of plane trees
in windows across the street, the leaping squirrels,
the wood pigeons, losing their eggs in flight,
shells smashing on the city's verge.

They want your sounds, the morning's rattle
of metallic shutters that fold away
Bart Simpson's sprayed-on head.
They want your vertigo brought
on by cranes that tower around you.
They want the grace of skateboarders gliding by.
They want whatever you find to admire.

And they'll take whatever else
you don't deserve to hear or see,
the park's public courts and the arcs
of tennis balls, whose rise and fall
they'll beat into a straightness,
then nail down in a crate.

Don't think they've gone. They're coming back again
to jimmy up the door and floor, prise out the walls
and pitch your box room into a skip.

They've bagged up your unwritten songs, fledglings
whose wings have been clipped, and, as they pack
tree shadows into tea chests,
your neighbours text *goodbye goodbye*
from the unrolling, distant street,

then retreat to the screens on their laps
in the acceptable flats where there is no space
to do anything but watch and eat.

Evening Teaching

Often it seems that the world
wants to stop it happening: the heating
creaks down to zero, or rises
to the tropics. The caretaker
shakes his keys on the threshold,
as if none of us really exist,
punches the lights out midway,
slams the door a batch of times,
while we assay our timetabled
session. Over and over, the caretaker
rattles back, practising his percussion,
until I call out, 'We're here till nine thirty.'
And the scribe leaps in, 'You mean
you'll be discussing this sort of thing
till nine thirty?' Yes, this sort of thing,
we go on discussing this sort of thing,
face to face, in the face of everything
that happened in the day,
perhaps death, love, easing splinters
from a finger with a needle
heated in the kettle's steam.
Now, all we ask is this space of chairs.
Then, come summer, we open windows
and, out in the grounds, a blackbird,
sometimes a nightingale, sings.

ask the heathland

in what measure shall I walk my grief?

for the cold day is not grief-stricken
being all sun, blue sky, bleached bark,
a fallen oak of moss plantations
over hollowings where carpenter bees
once tunnelled hidden runnels

in what measure shall I write my grief?

in frozen pools, the blond marrams of winter
wave from tussock islands

broken stems glint in lines
drawn on surface ice

in puddles and tracks
sole-sized glaciers swirl abstracts
over drowned needles of gorse

winter-white ling whispers *husky-husk*
its tongueless bells shift in the wind

a robin names its territory from the high birch
the gorse beckons a bumblebee
to rest on golden lips

in what measure can I compose my grief?

how to sing of bee larvae, mud-wrapped
under sand volcanoes, fed
by bee-butter, summer mothers?

in what measure can I count my grief?

maybe in the flitter
made by a woken adder, flicking
through the understory

walk in a wood after a long loneliness

you go into a wood, you find the place
where your father carved his childhood
there is the grain and the bole
the bark and the pen-knife's mark.
he walked on, but the tree remains, letters
widening with each year's ring

you search for clearings
where windflowers show white
and alexanders remember
their worldly journeyings
in bright green scatterings

you walk into a wood and stay there all night
you lie on leaf litter, hear
pheasants creaking beneath
a dark gloss of holly

you walk in a wood after a long loneliness

even now in the car, in the city,
you are in the wood, and the wood
is in you. remember? last night
you took my hand and

we were children, running up a bank,
grabbing onto a tangle of roots;
the tree above us leaned, sighed,
but it didn't fall

even when you walk the wood alone,
I'll find you by the stream below
the old carriage way, where late light
sends trees rippling into the water

The Machine

All they knew was that in the years
since it was what it had once been,

someone had painted a red square
on the staves and a mute green seven.

Someone had hammered a metal sheet
to the front, punctured it with eye-holes.

Some said it was a limber
that survived the war, its wheels intact.

Some guessed farm work, or talked
of a trench and a travelling forge.

The boys chalked letters
over the faded square of paint,

scratched eyes and hair onto the seven.
Not knowing its name, they named it

the machine and rumbled it into
the village's heart. Some nights,

laughing, shoulders to the wheel,
they shifted it onto the green.

Most mornings, the village played along,
saying the machine must have moved itself

to block the pub's yard, the church gate
or the baker's van, while the boys' eyes watered

from squinting through the rusty holes,
and their coughs ack-acked like guns.

Then, one night, while the boys slept,
the woods murmured to their fathers' words.

The hanger echoed with hammering,
dismembering. The boys searched the dens,

the common, the bostal path, the lythe,
thinking they would never find its parts again

though a few years later, the machine
assembled itself and came after them.

Night Walk with My Parents

We wanted to go out, they said,
even if it was only up the lane

to Coneycroft Hanger,
through the stream's flood,

which had drowned the front room
and left its water mark on plaster.

After they'd jumbled their muddy chairs
upstairs to huddle in the bedroom's mess,

they set off, with the cat following,
under the midnight moon

that sent its white light down
between beeches to cast shadows.

Then home to the damp walls, to dream
of the ditches drained of mud.

I barely listened. I wasn't there. But lately,
I follow their floodlit way to the wood.

They are brimful of young laughter,
as they slosh along Gracious Street.

Now I'm the elder and can't help shushing
when they splash past the cottages' closed eyes

or when they whistle for the cat, who jumps
across the lake of puddles, then turns back

to search for her own face down there
in the rippling moon.

To Wish on the Stone

we had to close our eyes, place a hand
on its chalk and walk backwards
around it three times three,
while the village dizzied away
to a whinny and a bark.

All night, I would dream of rolling
the wishing stone down the zigzag's flints,
right left, right left, as if I could
own the boundary's marker
and take possession of my wishes.

While I slept, blue woodsmoke
rose from chimneys and tangled
in the trees with the traveller's joy.

And while I slept, the salesmen came
out of the dark to stay, and the next day,
over breakfast, told a tale of leaving the pub
to climb the hill in their cups,
and then of zigzagging the stone round each curve
until they'd rolled it down to the village street,
from the Punfle path. Their shoes, eyelets clogged,
rimed with leaf mould and clay, stood by
as witnesses. My parents put it down to drink.
'You'll see,' I heard the men say,
'when you find the circle empty
where the stone once stood.'

These days, I go backwards and backwards, three times round,
and, though the wishing stone high on the Hanger
is now worn to a smaller mound,
the village still falls away and away,
to the echoes of a dog's bark, a thrush's song,
while blue woodsmoke meanders up again

from fires burning in hearths below,
until I question whether the stone rolls down
or whether the village rises through nests
and branches, lifted by blue smoke travelling
home to its family of trees.

The Bridge

Not being exact, I thought I couldn't be owned,
taking, as I did, a terrible pleasure in my hacked timbers.

My gaps were eyes where I glimpsed wagtails upending
in shallows or moorhens fussing with their lives.

I welcomed the wild chalk of children scratching
out their startled Picassos on my splintered surface.

Through my brokenness, I glimpsed waters running
under me, skeins that unravelled over

rocks and flints or pooled in meditative clouds,
so that I could gaze on the sky beneath.

Though I knew that, for many, I served only as a walkway
to the field of irises flying their yellow flags,

I would still inhale the hazy stink of meadowsweet
as if it were incense given for passage to the other side.

And when the dust of nettles flew over me
on the breeze and tried to settle, I let the seeds

into my softened wood to grow their rooting sinews.
And when the dogs dug their claws into me,

I was glad of the fierce and playful scuffle
of the living and the tread of the walkers' boots,

until the owners came, who axed the footpath sign
adrift, and hammered me into the true.

In all my fearful imaginings, I must confess that
I had not foreseen privacy, the limitations of repair,

or known how I would miss those foreign witnesses
to the long slow loveliness of my decay.

lines prompted by an old leather travel bag

knowing how he packed to a plan
and how we'd wear what we could on the drive out
      I gather up the village, fields and woods
to make a shirt but, lacking skill, I weave them
into a sheet, the warp, beech nuts flayed into thread,
the weft, a gleam of wild cherry bark, rippling
like the knuckled stream

      in the ward I fling the sheet over him
and, when he moves, meadows bend their stems
in shivers of poppy and vetch
          then, restless, he flattens the grass
with his weight, as cattle do before rain
      on days when children curl up
in the green bowl of a cow's warmth

      across him now the bosky track climbs to its goal
a day-moon, a hole in the sky's slub
of fraying trees, and when the map slips from him
      I settle the woodland across his shoulders
while he shrugs off the tree light, saying
      last night I dreamt that once all fields had names
      I take his hand and place it on the sheet
see here, I say, as he clutches swathes of hay
and lets them fall in switherings

      I am garrulous
as a jay, guessing at words
      until one sigh summons another
and stubble quills whisper of ditches and stiles
of greenfinches and the small weight of lapwings landing
      where have they gone? he asks
when I fold back the sheet
paths and coppices drift from my fingers

in his dreams, he names fields
        but in my dream, I twist hedgerows into a rope
lower him from the window
into the ticking car, then rip field names
        from the unravelling sheet, zip them into
the lining of the battered bag
        map-read its leather surface
                and so, we make our escape

In Trieste

we searched for James Joyce
upstairs in *Zara*, flipping through
suits on the menswear floor
where Nora's ghost
was cooking Jim a meal.

In Trieste
my father was a young soldier
tasting the water of life
draining bottled sunshine
after every explosion
and then longing
to get back there.

Years later,
the artists who lived in a barn
left a note saying 'Gone to Trieste',
propped against eggshells
smashed in their cups.

'Driven there spontaneously,'
my father said enviously,
fingering his unpaid bill,
as if he was Stanislaus Joyce,
hearing Jim and Nora
were off to the opera,
bleeding him dry again
and, what's worse, had
left him the washing-up.

Jane Austen's Visitor

I am toothless, white haired, twenty-one.
I was fifteen, though no one counted the years,
but me. I hid in the corn like a deer.
When I raised my head to see,
the press gang pounced and netted me.

At the end, I lay on the stilled deck.
Under my eyelids, fiery ships flashed.
Scorched hands stuck to broken timbers.
For days, I was a log that no one could flog
into obedience. At last, the captain set me loose,
a dog limping homewards.

Now the door creaks, as I push my way in.
My tongue can't find the words I want.
Bread. A slice of ham. All that comes:
a toothless flip-flap of lips, a dying fish.

I watch the marvel of clean muslin arms
and the little curl escaping from her cap.
Her pen drifts over small inky sheets.
She scissors out islands of script.
Captain Benwick, Captain Wentworth, Admiral Croft.
She takes long pins and tacks the new words
over old sentences. I gather the cut paper,
squinny at her through its holes.

I could stop your ears with my story, I say.

She stares me out through the paper mask.
I hear her sigh. *I can't write what I don't know.*
There's an apple pie in the kitchen. Eat it, please.
Then, I must let you go.

Studio mirror: the maid speaks

(after Christ in the House of Mary and Martha by Velázquez)

The globe of garlic is broken
into cloves. Its root bristles,
unearthed to tell of wilting flowers

and leaves soured to pungency in heat.
The mortar's metal, the four dead fish,
the light of our eight eyes,

my mother's earring heavy in my ear,
all solder me into the pattern of the gleam.
These eggs I've peeled and their dish's glaze

catch my gaze more than varnished figures.
The pepper twists into a memento mori.
The old woman's beaded bracelet threads trinities

of red and white, blood and lost love,
and warns me not to linger before the dark glass,
but to grip the things of this world,

to run out of the shuttered rooms,
with no envy for foot-washers,
no desire to sit listening to anyone.

Dalí among the cactuses

Dalí walks the hills of Spain
spying on families of cactus

what he sees makes his moustaches curl

a desiccated leaf, the drips
from spines forming
weather systems of the self

a hedge of living statues
fencing the heat,
arm to arm, edging
down the mountain's noon

all the years a cactus grows are
inside the green grotesque
of their sweet watery limbs

a horse mimes a cactus,
deadbeat on the golden stone

a cactus mimes a horse, all ears,
nose to sky, tail withered

Dalí, among the cactuses,
straps a dried paw to his wrist,

holds the cactus to his ear,
hears its tick, its exhalation

he shakes the stopped watches,
dried ovals, bodies of memory,

then drapes them on stone

everywhere we walk he's scattered
pointing hands and melting clocks

time paused, growing, passing

Time slip

The man enters with an axe. He is whispering
to himself or maybe talking to the axe,
as if it knows him, knows his nose,
knows his arm's length and can see his
naked toes. He swings it into the heart
of the room at some invisible trunk
that once grew up to the sky, through
the roof before the roof was there, when the air
was bare-headed, unceilinged, before
the plaster rose bloomed. The blade
cuts through the space so easily that the axe
flies into the rug, splits its red wool trellis.
The handle beckons his hand. But he resists,
stands where a tree once stood, raises
his eyes, and then his hands, his bare arms,
and mimes his way back to the present.

Sweet Woodruff

Remember sweet woodruff in armfuls
stuffed between the mattress's linen
or piled under hemp?

A scratchy softness for a body to lie on
in the ache between work and morning,
a dream floating in farm dust
before waking to straw lines of thatch.

How comforting the gathering and strewing
in the days when woodruff scented our skin
and ticked on in its crackle,
a rough life slowing to a dryness of stems.

When the body twitched and itched,
we could look for hope in a garden.

Ancestors, take us now
to a bed of sweet woodruff,
and, in the cutting and gathering,
soothe us with thoughts of a cure.

In the touch of our hands on a plant,
whisper your lore.

Comfort

Where there is pain,
a knocked arm, a bruised knee,
search for knitbone, bruisewort,

comfrey swayed by bees
in a warm breeze,
the mind longing for ease.

The Night Table

(after Edip Cansever)

A woman who can't sleep puts the moon
on the table in its halo of cloud,
goes out to the garden to cut
woodruff and jugs a sheath
of its tall stems for the table.
She puts the agony of doing wrong
on the table. She questions the meaning
of three and puts her question on the table.
She takes a torch and puzzles out
woundwort in the wilderness of the hedge.
In the kitchen, lit by the moon's lamp,
she counts off red flowers. Woundwort, she says,
healer of cuts, mender of skin, cure me now.
Even though marigolds close their faces
to the dark, she pounds their orange petals
with a pestle. Then, she calls dawn to the table
to sweep up the curled seed moons
and scatter them onto a bed of earth.
The woman prays for sleep and puts
her prayer on the table. The table creaks.

Terrace Ghosts

Neighbour, did you hear my man smashing plates?
Or did the clatter of your tin bath mask the sound?

Neighbour, did you press your ear to the wall,
as mine is now, listening to your water pour?

That chuckle is the coal bucket's rattle,
that whistle is the kettle's breath,

that fizz you hear, my iron on the sheets,
that heavy slosh I hear, you lazing there.

Neighbour, I'll stoke the stove, if you'll rise, dripping,
to lay your palm against the chimney's heat.

on seeing a drift of blackthorn in April's haze

some say we can't travel back
in time but can fly to the future

white flowers grow into blue sloes
seed-stones fall to the ground

a blackthorn winter inhabits spring

when the hedge-mist sings beside fields
I'm pulled to the edge of years

thinking birds will nest forever
in thickets of the past, not counting the notes
nor hearing the song thin

Question

To find the answer,
melt a shaft
        in the ice sheet.
Drill down
        five hundred thousand years.
Then twist,
        helter-skelter,
through miles
        of vertical ice,
                down and down
        through the white darkness
            to ask
the hidden waters
        of the lake.

At the Stone Chamber of an Ancient Village

I wonder what the old herdsmen
knew of impositions of holiness
and why rainwater in a stone with a hollow,
once a quern or prop for a post,

now translates to a bowl of blessing.
A druid priest, yellow fluorescent jacket
over hooded linen robe, summons
the four winds to bless the bride

in her found wedding dress and trainers
and to bless the groom, tweeded out
like a young Edwardian farmer,
while the witnesses hold hands,

make almost another round house
of their arched arms and baggy fleeces
to pray to the spirits of bramble and bird,
their feet planted on the roof

of the underground chamber. Inside,
the gap in earth lends light
to luminous moss. A woman tells us
how she spent the night here once,

'What we saw, I cannot say,
but when we called the spirits,
the moss grew greener, brighter,
and we were changed.'

Through the earth's gap, we hear
the wind shaking towers of foxgloves,
rattling gorse and heather,
while clouds fall through

the lantern of this grave pantheon
into its pool. Now the sky moves
under earth, and the present blows in,
a magpie's feather, petals of a wild rose

loosened from the bride's bouquet,
a phone's ringtone, the song of the druid party,
who, above us, welcome the rain,
turn laughing faces to the storm.

lockdown bluebells

flower muskily under oak and hazel
in the wood row by the river

walkers out for an hour
tread the same path

their feet wearing
stems into a shine of sap

that might have stiffened lace
in plague years past

two deer tread lightly
through the blue, leave

barely a bruise,
only the arc

of a delicate leap
in the heady air

we take breaths
of bluebell

but their scent
will not soften our fear

of touching the gloss
of others here

in these blue hours
we start

from one another
like deer

above ourselves

a man is stretching bubbles
outside Tate Modern
stretching them between sticks

elasticising liquid
into airy globes
which escape and fly

along and over and into
the lines of tourists
and giggling, fencing children

here they are tumbling
through the air as if
the soul has been drawn

from a bucket of soap
and set free though
often grown-ups feared

we would get above
ourselves but not as these
towers have got above us

but as these bubbles
who ride the breeze
to the scrubbed white bark

of planted birches
not caring that a touch
may be the death of them

To sing of soap in desperate times

in spite of palm plantations,
felled rainforests and effluence,
in spite of plastic dispensers,
in spite of nitrogylcerine,
in spite of a name that categorises
life-long dramas

to sing of soap is to sing *al-galy*,
wood ash that lends its name to alkali,
to sing rainwater and to sing oils,
olive, vegetable, sesame, and not to mourn
an absence of tallow – for who wants
to rub the fat of a cow on their skin?

to sing some soap names but not others,
to sing Pears, Dove and Lifebuoy,
but not Imperial Leather, a name saddled with empire,
whose legacy refuses to be washed down the plughole

to sing of the soap my daughter gave me,
nettle and seaweed, astringent shore,
field margin, seawater, kelp, ribbon of nori

to sing soap is to sing my grandmother lathering
a slip of Palmolive for skin and laundry and then
to sing the green unrinsed forgetfulness
streaking her long white hair

to sing my sister's gift of a bar of soap
is to sing a fourth dimension containing
the bloom of two lavender bushes

to sing soap is to sing a child
sifting pink stars through fingers
in a bucket of water and soapwort
at the living museum

to sing soap was to choose on days
when the French market still came to town
from *les savons de Marseille,*
fenouil, citron, or *muguet des bois,*

to sing soap is to sing Happy Birthday twice
congratulating yourself like a prime minister

or to watch Gloria Gaynor washing
her hands, singing 'I will survive'
for twenty glorious seconds of being alive

An Hour's Walk

Once there was going to work,
the street welcome, like privacy,
a place she could find herself walking,
where words like *nice weather*
carried only one meaning.

Homewards, she dawdled through the park,
lingered over plants, smuggled
their names across the threshold.
In those days, it was the faraway
of her eyes that made him Mao,
assaulter of the kind of greenery
that cannot survive a vase.

Now, day is a closed front door,
and she can only say sorry for
catching her own fingers in the jamb.

Tomorrow's life is an ordered list
because she can never remember, can she,
to set the table before peeling the carrots.
It's not him. It's the government
who advises a routine of ritual
and outside contact to be virtual.

Days into lockdown, she does nothing
but look zero in the mirror's face.

Once she loved to spread a cloth
for her mother and put dandelions
in a jar for their shaggy heads of gold,
their pom-pom glow on linen.

One hour allowed in the silent street.
Step after step, and the old names come back.
Lion's teeth and *piss-the-bed*.

Sunlight wraps her in her mother's frock.
Seeds float from a clock of mist
in the tarmac's crack.
Their almost touch returns
a lore, once known by heart,
to the tongue's tip:
dock for a sting, self-heal for cuts,
borage for courage.

The Sears and Roebuck Sheet as Scrubs Bag

In nineteen seventy, my mother-in-law
bought a Sears and Roebuck sheet
from a New England store.
We often slept on that sheet.
Her never known grandchildren
slept on it too until it wore and tore.

Now, in this time of the virus,
I thread my sewing machine,
alive to my mother-in-law's
presence. We met twice only.
First at lunch and last in hospital.
Sometimes contraries are true.

I am fond of her and never knew her.
They say she found choosing
an agonising act. In Sears, her fingers
stretch to feel the softness, as she doubts
the design and considers
the durability of polycotton.

She could not have foreseen that I
would use her sheet and later cut it up,
or that I'd feel sad as the scissors tore
through the blue leaves, or that
the pattern, which perhaps surprisingly
we liked, patched itself into our history.

She couldn't know that the sheet's head
would become a drawstring's case,
or that selvedge would be pressed
to selvedge in a seam, tensions
tightening and loosening, or that
quick dry polycotton is best for scrubs.

Repurposed, the sheet flaps
from our line, in a guise of laundry bags,
matching the new blue of near empty skies.
A Sussex breeze balloons the fabric
into whirling shadows over grass.
I try not to think about death,

as I follow Christine out of Sears,
back to the lake and forest cabins.
She is as slender as my daughter. Canoes
still rock at their Rockywold moorings.
Did she choose well? Yes, I say as I unfold
the sheet, and she smooths it over the bed.

Through a glass darkly

Here is a WhatsApp film of deer running. Your scene in my hand, in my head. Here is your painting on a studio floor. Here is a sand martin flying into a sand cliff. Replay. Here is your girlfriend in the snow, in a headscarf, in an old Soviet spa. Replay. Here you are dressed as Jamiroquai dancing through a hallway in Peckham Rye. Replay. Several times. Sigh. Here are your paints. Here are your plants. Here is a crown of cauliflower cooked in coconut cream. Here you are with your hair dyed pink. Here are your octopus arms playing the drums. Here you are pulling a face on the band's merch, fierce Viking of our ancestry. Here is a mole digging out our car with a shovel nose and tiny hands. And here I am, herding the mole away. Here is a snail, vision blurred and monochrome: grief. For indistinct fluorescent banded sight, my tear-blurred eyes, see through the pinprick gazes of a clam. But to reprise. Here is a film of your legs in a garden pond seen through your eyes. Here is the sound of a thrush, singing the streets of South London. Here are ransoms glowing in a wood. No one taught you the words we used to learn and their strange poetry. In these days of social distance, I must admit that knowing how to use WhatsApp is a greater emotional hit. But missing you, the actual you, the both of you, I want to quote old words from a lost faith, *now we see through a glass darkly, then face to face*. At each electric bleep, this is my paraphrased prayer. *Now darkly, soon face to face*.

Elegy for the Closeness of London

(reflections on a day in May 2019 in the virus year 2020)

Last year, in London, before the lockdown,
I passed Sue's poem in the underpass,
crossed the river and walked to Queen's Square.
It was a May Bank Holiday weekend
and the poetry of women drew me there.

In the workshop, we weren't scared to be
close around the long table, or to share
our inspirations, seeking the breath
of a kind of divination.

We wrote about the city, country, town
the room of our lives. Outside a crane
hauled a room over our building and let it
dangle there, while the homeless slept on, on
benches among bluebells and late primroses.
Such was London in its contradictions.

Last year in London, before the lock-down,
lunch was a sandwich in Bloomsbury Square
where foreign lovers basked in the warmth
of each other's language. Under the shade
of a lime, a group practised Tai Chi,
their breathing careful, consciously in sync.

Walking on, I glimpsed three white-robed women,
sitting on plastic chairs in the backyard
of a spa. Laughing heads close, they passed round
a cigarette, like some secret gossip shared.
No fear of another's breath made them scared.

In Stanfords, I met with my dear friend
and stroked the name on her novel's spine.
Since she died, it has become my ritual
to touch the covers of her books

as if my fingers will restore her, and
writing's blessing resurrect her here
to walk towards me through the stacks.
Last year, I had no fear of touch, and often
thought I saw her through the crowd and ran
to hug her, but she'd gone, a swirl of blonde,
disappearing down the stairs, turning only
once to say, 'You stay. I've gone. I've gone.'

In Trafalgar Square, a man chalked national
flags onto a grid. He and the pavement
knew all the designs of the world by heart.

A woman with a megaphone drew me
to her protest. She was Sudanese and said:
'We have mothers. We have children,
We want education, sanitation.
We have rivers. We have deserts.
We want to vote. We want an end to war.'
Shoulder to shoulder with the Sudanese men,
I listened to her litany. Her breath.
If someone touched, I didn't shy away.
The golden living statues, elves on sticks,
grew rapt by her words, as did a silvered
Charlie Chaplin, so moved, he gave a bow.

But I was on my way to Martin Parr's
Made in Britain show at the NPG,
on its last day. And once there, I was haunted
by the unphotographed, the unshowy,
who don't dress up in costumes, don't hunt
with hounds, kayak at night, salsa dance,
ditch dive, go twitching in a crowd, who don't
join winter swimmers on Brighton beach,
don't cloak themselves in red and white
on St George's Day, and don't play
rugby, save lives or go to Goodwood. Now
we must become the people who are not
in Martin Parr's photos, lonely figures

walking distant paths, evasive, dressing
up in gloves and masks. We must know
oneness now in a different way. But then
when I left, meandering into the brush
of tourists, heedless and happy, the flash
of phones caught me off-guard, in the smoke
and the bangs of the thunderbolts thrown,
and then fire flared at the entry to the Mall,
and the golden elves on air, climbed down,
and their gold cloaks shimmered as they moved
towards the flames, and we, the crowd, became
a flashing mini-storm of Zeuses, following.

'It's only an Uber exploding,' they said.
Only an Uber, a life, a living.
'The driver's out. He's OK.' The wisdom
of the crowd was organic now, moving forward
for the best shot, no thought of terror,
only to catch each other in the shock
and smoke and the comfort of sirens.
An ambulance, the police and the fire
engines rolled in, blocking the road.
'We want public services. We want law,'
the Sudanese woman shouted in the smoke.
There was no space between us, but we didn't
care. It was only an Uber exploding
in the centre of the city, but fear
swept me. 'We have rivers, we have deserts.'

Strange that day should seem so precious, now
that we have become the people not in
Martin Parr's photographs. The flags are washed
from the paving. The crane that lifted
the room of our lives is still. But on that
May day, I walked over Hungerford Bridge
to find my husband at Gabriel's Wharf,
and it seemed that the murmurs around us
were the music of the hosts of heaven,
and pizza and beer, a communion.

Elbow to elbow, close as breath, the young
were swiping right, swiping left, meeting
new lovers by the river, holding paper cups,
plastic bottles, dirty change, trusting somehow
that our faulty, arty, dancing, snap-happy
international London would go on,
and we partygoers would jostle each other,
breathing, touching, posing as if we could
be close in Martin's photos forever.

After an evening's writing in the shed

I stumble back from the garden's dark,
to red lanterns, flamed purple
by the kitchen light.

Indoors, I write to you about the fuchsia,
tapping out words into white space.

In your mind's eye, I see the winter flowering,
the persistent petal glow despite the cold.
Characters slip away over electric snow.
And I want to say, *Don't go. Not yet.*
If you're not there, who will care
about the fuchsia's late fire?
Who will care to know?

The Summoner of Birds

(i.m. H.D.)

A rounded woman, her hair up
in a sea-coloured net, wearing a blue dress,
a white apron, carrying a bowl on her hip,
walks out of now, walks out of time,
walks out onto the pebbles, steps
over the winch's chain to the wash
of small waves to summon a gyre
of gulls and their cries.
                              She pauses
where the stream pours into the sea,
lifts the bowl from her hip
and, in one curved move, flings
knuckle bones, neck joints, spareribs,
arrows of seabass, sole and cod
into the air to drop in a moment's fall
till snatched by the beaks of the gulls
and carried up again, while sand pipers
pick the beach clean, and the winch
weighs down the scene.

Then, comes a winged giant along the Todden
threatening death, but underneath
an actor works his wings.
                              Mostly, what I miss
in these soon after days, is our talk,
what I would have said, what you
would have made of this. The shadows
of things, of gulls, of paper wings, of bones
play out on the harbour's shore,
with one witness less. And now,
the woman in the blue dress
picks up the empty bowl and returns
to the inn. The giant folds his wings.
Even with you gone, I shape this story,
and ask, what do you make of this?

The Wake

You waited out the cold
as if you too were a plant.
You saw buds stall in snow.

Ungrown: the flow under beeches,
then the tilt of bluebells in grass,
and the quick contingencies,

soapwort, stitchwort, windflowers,
wild cherry above archangel,
cowslips clinging to a bank.

In the mind's eye: bottles roll
on the lawn, and tables
are cleared of their glasses.

This is what you waited for:
to step over the threshold,
as a mourner will step through

a doorway, to pause on the road
alone in the quiet rain
with one bird singing.

Your Poem

I practise your poem
for the reading that you
can no longer give.

I strain to keep my voice clear,
no leaves choking the grate,
no dam breaking the stream.

While I rehearse,
next door's dogs
yodel at the gale,

howl in their loneliness,
wolves scratching
at the everyday wall.

At St Erth

That time we waited with you at the station,
you were as soignée as ever, wearing
a black velvet coat that you'd had relined.
As women love to do, we talked about the lining,
its shininess, the long splash of red flowers,
a hint of wildness inside startling
the conventions of the plain smart coat.

Walking the Path Again

(i.m. H.D.)

Our talk paced the grass, or fell on the track,
streaks of light through budding trees, primroses
and riffs of windblown shade, the voice of rusted
bracken rustling over new. Word after word
we walked, two families, our spoken thoughts
a measure of milestones, way markers, stiles
and fingerposts, as if the rungs of gates
were staves marking notes of a song until
we reached the cave of pillars and wood,
wind buffeting the walls and Cornish air
shining in the granite glint. Retracing,
I can't recall now what it was we said.
Maybe the step by step by step was all,
Maybe rhyme can fill no gap; the gap is all.

Here we are, back on the same track, us two,
the children grown, you gone, September
of another year. To me, the bloody
fuchsias seem to cry, toss their tear-shaped
heads in the Cornish wind, though I guess
you might have seen them not as emblems
of grief but acts of setting seed. We leaf
through the visitors' book and find the date
of that other walk and a shock, a glimpse
of what you saw the day we didn't see
you writing in the book. And, as your friend,
I won't quote your words, for they are yours
not mine, a haiku flaring from the page,
a glint, a gleam, a generosity.

We climb a stone seat in the church's porch
to see the swallows' autumn nest, the young
with open beaks, wanting their mother
as our babies, born the same week, wanted us.

A seal glides into my thought, as we'd seen
her when the children called, 'A seal, a seal.'
The roundness of her wakeful head cleaves
the tide, leaves a whirl, which vanishes. And
yet nothing remains still. From Gurnard's Head,
to Zennor to Wicca pool, the children call
'A seal, a seal', as she floats and disappears
like our talk which dived deep under cliffs,
then, rose in laughing waves and swam along,
to surface often in the water's sun.

The Conversation

(i.m. H.D.)

Now our words need a new measure of time,
syllables for seconds, sonnets for minutes,
epics for hours – this is our café society,
as if the café will never close and the steps
from the café will never tip us out
on to Trafalgar Square, to hurry across the wet stones,
with the gold of our talk glinting round our feet,
the largesse of winter scattering our reflections
into the tears of the fountain's mist, which falls
and rises to the lit-up windows, gathering
in the bare-armed trees. There we are, leaving
the coffee spoons and teaspoons on saucers,
hurrying away to our separate evenings,
walking out among the languages of the world
which find no true word for the talk of women,
unless, dear friend, I name our talk for you,
a light that shimmers along city streets
and out along the lanes of great souled hills.

Siskin

They say if you teeter at the edge
of the lake with a fishing net,
you may dredge up bottles
that a writer threw in at the party,
watching them float, then drown
as water filled their bodies.

They say the women
were dressed as yellowly
as azaleas and tossed in the corks
to bob along, then slow
in duck weed.

On the day before
the last day I ever saw you,
dragonflies shone in lines
of turquoise, hovered over
the lake's green darkness,
and its drowned may.

I didn't want
to imagine you dying,
and so I pulled us both
into the party, while
a siskin sang in the trees.

Look at them/us unfolding the deck chairs
and fixing their frames.
There was the sound of an argument,
dogs barking, the hiss of adders.

Give them/us, the protagonists,
the heat of the garden wall,
anger and politics, a love triangle,
antagonists. We/they will play the triangle

with a tiny spanner and listen
to its delicate water music,
while we drink champagne.

Then, imagine, years later,
a jeroboam rising
from the mud wrack
to tell the argument,
as if it lived again.

Daedalus over the Downs

A man puts his arm through the harness of his wing,
snaps the buckles fast, takes the weight of canvas,
and hears the baffled slings sing in his creaking ear.

Helmeted, he edges his way slope-wards,
breathing in the old chalkland scent. Over there where
the stunted families of hawthorn point windbitten arms
to the air, he runs down the curve as children do,
harum-scarum, running to fly.

He is a father, a new husband, then he's eighteen again,
his back against the vetch and creeping thistle,
a lovely girl warm beside him on the crushed thyme.
If only he could stop there, but he can't, he's fifteen
sitting on a log, smoking a secret spliff, he is ten weeping
for his dead dog, his only friend, and then his feet slip on chalk,
skid him into the launch.
       Now the arc of fabric fills
with air. So often, he's wanted to ride a current
that will carry him to a truer view of the Downs.
White scars of paths drawn by foot or hoof
jitter towards him, juggling the scarps
then hiding themselves in the copse's caverns of yew.
And, gliding on, he catches the signal glints
from troughs, drenched coffins, man-sized baths,
that flash back his red half-moon on mirror
water. And, up over again, where Didling church
marks the lane, the green corrugations
of barn roofs ripple away from him. Yellow fields
slant up to patch the lines below.
He's swearing with relief,
laughing now, talking to the air, to the skylarks,
as he sees his shadow wing skimming the blackthorn,
caressing the view in a way that he never could,
when he'd trailed his childhood hands over the scarp

and pressed his fingers into every valley of plaster
on the dusty contour map in the village hall.

Though his eyes water in the wind,
surely he has the measure of it now,
the Devil's Jumps humping their bell barrows
over the earth, their ancient burrowings.
But it was nothing like this, he thinks, nothing
like riding thermals, so far up that he can't
see the golden mouths of the buttercups
or, below him on the path, the ragged feather,
which has floated down, as his son's feather did,
to the white chalk beneath his dangling feet.

Gate on the Downs

A cold June evening. Our grown children
newly gone again to their cities.

Up here, a pair of nesting jays lose their shyness,
flit in and out of the hawthorn's tunnel.

A buzzard puzzles the copse with wary turnings,
fogged by shreds of whirling smoke.

I want to know whether the blue-grey streak
on the other side is really the Channel,

a cloud hedge or a passing bruise of weather,
and why the stile must be a cross of steps,

and why the airy wire fences need to fence
the rattle of the seeding cowslips.

I need landmarks like this metal trough, where
sheep lap up the changing heavens.

I want to skip the scudding mist,
the slippery steep, and lark up and over

in a hover to a singing sky.
But I can't. And so, this post, a star

of signs planted in its cairn of stones
may as well be my guide

to restricted bridleways, permitted footpaths.
I follow the finger pointing

to a fenceless unnecessary gate
alone on the scarp's edge.

On the other side, a slope of orchids, darkly splashed,
falls away from the chalk scarred view.

No need for barriers on these open hills,
but someone set this gate among the nettles.

And, though we could so freely go around
or over, something forces us through.

What the chair saw

was a figure, moving towards it. What the chair heard was weeping. What the chair felt was movement as it swayed through the air. What the chair sensed was a jolt as its legs hit the floor. The chair noted blue paint and scuff marks. The light fell a different way and cast the shadow of a question mark over the chair. The chair wanted to ask where in the room it was now. Even in that moment, the chair missed the table.

The chair wished to say that no one should stand on its seat. Yet, the chair creaked under two bare feet. The chair felt lighter under the shadows of two soles. The chair creaked under two more feet. The chair murmured. The chair felt the weight of one body, holding another. How would it stand that double weight? The chair thought it would buckle, that its wood would split. But the second body kept on holding on to the first. Two feet stayed on the chair's seat. And then there were four. Then none.

The chair longed for its companions. The chair felt the atmosphere lighten. Later the chair joined the other chairs at the table, where the meal went along as usual.

The Clumsinesses

You know when you said what I said that she said that he said, and then I dropped the bottles? They slid through my hands, explosive. Cola fizzed on sandy boards, as the sea outside battered rocks. Often, I think that was the first clumsiness. But there must have been others. Some joyful, such as crayoning inside a book over print and pictures.

In the era of the second clumsiness, I was my own poltergeist – knocking mirrors from walls, scorching skin on the cooker. Once, when the iron leaked, a flame ran down the lead and sparked fire, while the washing machine flooded my feet. I came close to my own electrification, which could have been the last clumsiness. The worst kind: careless talk, the hurtful word. What stains they leave, like cola on the wooden floor, with no sea to wash away the outline. In the broken mirror, I glimpse fragments of the self as a stick of glue, trying to paste together an eye here, a tooth there.

In the era of the third clumsiness, the day slows though the hour runs faster. I have broken the glass of minutes. Sand spills out over the table, small map of somewhere. And I hold a translucent cup in my hand, gaze at light visible through thin china, observe Japanese flowers and cracks of gold leaf. This time, I place the cup on the table slowly, then fill it to the brim.

The Tile

Where I work, at the garden's end,
birds make nests in the cladding, and so,
in spring, one corner of this shed will sing
for sure. Here, ant colonies rot timbers;
then ants busy their way in, swirling eggs
under the door's gap. Flies dot dot
the books, and postcards of paintings
won't be pinned but float floorwards
to drift among scuffling drafts.

I still don't learn. I invite more in,
like this piece of tile from Lisbon,
bought for two Euros from a stall
in Santa Clara market, and before that
struck from the façade of a house in Coimbra,
and before that painted by the brush
of a seventeenth century workman
whose feet felt an earthquake's tremor,
whose eyelashes blinked pigment,
and whose fingers lengthened over years
to the work of the design. A drop of ginja,
the spitting of the cherry stone,
the morning's dream of Delft not yet dowsed
from him by the well-bucket's water.

I prop the broken pitted azulejo
on the *Big Book of Questions*
and study it for hours.

Here are the chisel marks,
here the not quite straight lines,
and here a blue squiggle, a mouth in a cloud,
quizzing me from the fired surface.

Landings

All day, the rook flies
its shadow self over the half-moons
of the tussocks' shade.

Sparrows scatter grey dabs
on grass,
                    moments
that rise, then vanish.

Now cirrus sends its quivering
over the barley.

Say that the sky will give up its own
as gently as this rook's shadow falls

on the field, wing under wing, tail under tail,
when the bird lands to feed and caw

and nod, at home with its kin
among the heaped clouds of sheep,
its shadow stowed at its feet.